STEP-BY-

MAKING

CARDS

BB 1856 **973263** 8004

D0511590

Class: 745.5941

CHARLOTTE STOWELL
ILLUSTRATED BY JIM ROBINS

KING*f*ISHER

KINGFISHER
Kingfisher Publications Plc
New Penderel House
283–288 High Holborn
London WC1V 7HZ

First published by Kingfisher
Publications Plc 1995
This edition published 2000

10 9 8 7 6 5 4 3 2 1

1TR/1199/SC/((HBM)/128JMA

Copyright © Kingfisher Publications
Plc 2000

All rights reserved. No part
of this publication may be
reproduced, stored in a retrieval
system or transmitted by any
means, electronic, mechanical,
photocopying or otherwise,
without the prior permission
of the publisher.

A CIP catalogue record for this
book is available from the British
Library.

ISBN 1 85697 326 3

Series editor: Deri Robins
Series designer: Ben White
Illustrator: Jim Robins
Photographer: Steve Shott
Cover designer: Terry Woodley

Printed in Hong Kong/China

CONTENTS

Pembroke Branch Tel. 6689575

WHAT YOU NEED

To make the cards in this book, collect together a basic kit like the one shown here. Some of the projects require a few extra bits and pieces – check by reading through the step-by-step instructions before you begin.

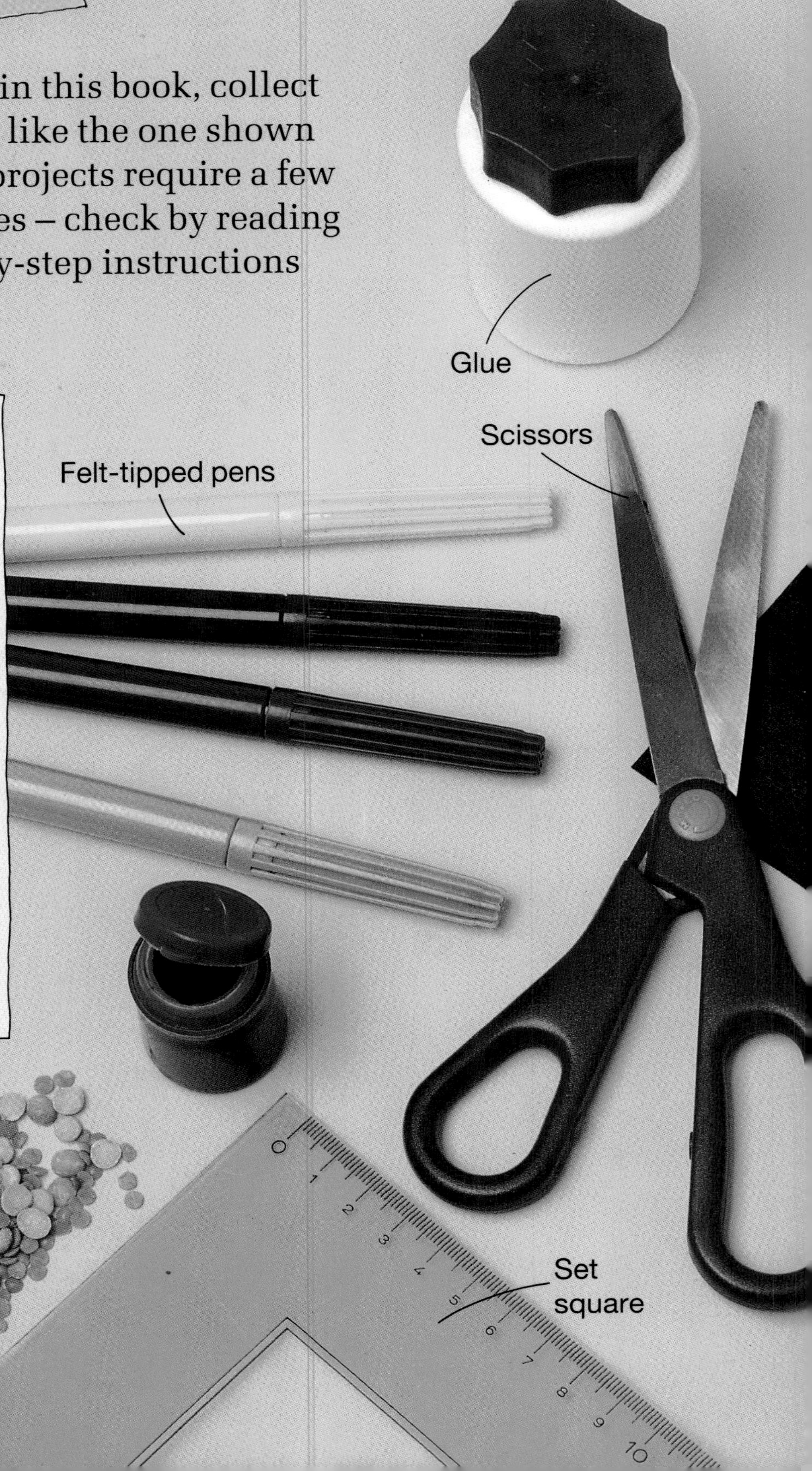

Glue

Scissors

Paper and Card

The main thing you'll need is a good supply of thin card. You can make cards from paper, but you'll have to fold each sheet in half to double the thickness before you begin – otherwise they'll be too floppy to stand up!

Coloured paper, tissue, crêpe and wrapping paper, old magazines and wallpaper can all be used to decorate your cards.

Felt-tipped pens

Dried beans and lentils

Foam block

Set square

Tools of the Trade

You'll need a pair of scissors, a set square, a craft knife, a metal ruler, paint brushes and pencils, and a cutting board to protect your table – a big piece of thick card, wood or formica is ideal.

Always handle craft knives very carefully, and only use them when an adult is around to help.

Paints and Glue

For sticking paper and card together, use white glue (PVA) or children's UHU™.

Most of the cards in this book were decorated by cutting shapes out of paper and gluing them to the design. You could also colour your cards with paints or felt-tipped pens.

Paper and card

Paper-fasteners

Metal ruler

Coloured pencils

Craft knife

Brushes

Bits and Pieces

Other useful materials include foam blocks for printing, a needle and cotton, an elastic band, and paper-fasteners.

Fabric scraps, wool, dried beans and lentils, kitchen foil and many other bits and pieces can be used to make collage cards.

Poster paints

Kitchen foil

HINTS & TIPS

The cards in this book are all easy to make – they're also a lot more fun to send than ones you've bought from the shops! Just take your time, and follow all the instructions carefully. Before you start, read the tips below.

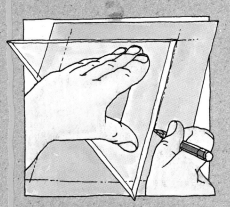

Measuring Up

It's best to use a set square rather than a ruler when you're measuring your cards. If you use the right-angled edges to help you draw the corners, your cards will look very professional.

Folding

Folding card is much easier if you *score* it first. Measure and draw the fold line, using a ruler and a pencil. Then press the nib of an empty ballpoint pen along the line, using a metal ruler as a guide.

Illustrating

To illustrate your cards, you could simply paint a design on the front. Or, cut shapes from coloured paper, and glue them down. You can even make collage cards, using all kinds of bits and pieces.

The pictures on the right show three different ways of illustrating the same design. Each illustration was done on a separate piece of card, then cut and glued onto a piece of folded card. This is called 'mounting'.

Painted card

Collage card

Card decorated
with paper
shapes

PRINTING CARDS

Use small shapes to print borders. They are also a good way to build up pictures – for example, a simple oval shape was repeated to make the petals of the sunflower opposite.

1

Draw a simple shape onto a piece of thick foam or polystyrene, using a felt-tipped pen. Cut the shape out carefully with a craft knife.

2

Cut several squares or rectangles from thin card, each a little bit smaller than the folded cards you have already prepared.

Printing is a quick way to make a big batch of cards – at Christmas, for example, or when you want to invite a lot of friends to a party. Before you start printing, cut out all the cards you need. Fold them in half, and put them to one side.

3 Pour some thick poster paint into a saucer. Dip the printing shape into the paint, and press it firmly onto one of the squares of card.

4 Keep dipping and printing until you have enough pictures. When they're dry, mount them onto the front of the folded cards.

MAKING ENVELOPES

Your cards will look extra special if you send them in your own home-made envelopes! The instructions given here will work for any size. Try printing the backs and borders with brightly-coloured paints (see pages 8–9), and sealing the flaps with glue or sticky paper shapes.

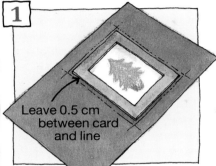

1 Leave 0.5 cm between card and line

Lay your folded card on a big sheet of coloured paper. Draw around it, making the line 0.5 cm wider on all sides.

2

Draw another rectangle under the first one. It should be exactly the same width, but about 0.5 cm shorter.

Why send plain envelopes when printed ones look so stunning?

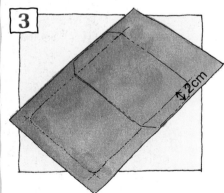

3 2 cm

Draw curves inside the bottom two corners. Add two 2 cm flaps at each side of the top rectangle, as shown.

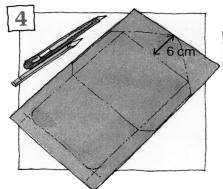

4

Draw a triangle at the top, making it at least 6 cm deep so that it overlaps the bottom rectangle when folded.

6 cm

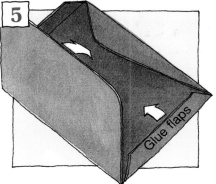

5

Cut out the shape with a craft knife. Fold all the lines inwards, and glue the bottom rectangle over the side flaps.

Glue flaps

BIRTHDAY SHAPES

Here are some very simple cards that just need a little folding and cutting. The colourful numbers would make great birthday cards for friends, brothers or sisters – or how about making the leaping dolphin for an animal-loving mum or dad?

Folded edge

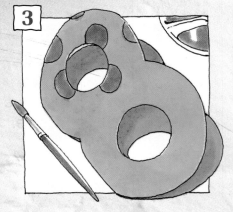

Number Cards

Draw a number onto a piece of folded card. One side must touch the folded edge.

Cut out the number, making sure you don't cut through the folded part of the design.

Paint the card, or decorate it by gluing down shapes cut from coloured paper.

Stand-ups

Cut out a rectangle from card, and lightly draw a line across the middle in pencil.

Draw a design, with the top part just above the middle line. Colour with paints or paper collage.

Cut around the top part with a craft knife. Then score along the line and fold backwards.

The train was made in the same way as the number cards, but the folded edge is at the top, not at the side.

The ark and dolphin both have a simple stand-up shape that can easily be cut out with a craft knife.

SURPRISE!

Always keep the main picture of a surprise card well hidden – just hint at what's underneath, as we've done here with the tip of the tiger's ears!

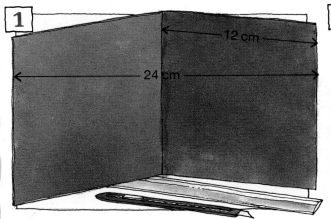

1 Measure a 24 x 12 cm rectangle onto a piece of green card, and cut it out. Score a line down the middle, and fold the card in half.

2 Draw a simple bush shape on the front of the card, as shown in the picture. Cut along this line, using a craft knife or scissors.

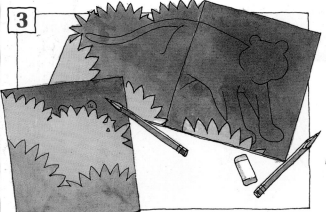

3 Close the card, and lightly sketch the tip of the tiger's ears on the inside, using a pencil. Open the card again, and draw the rest of the tiger's body.

4 Use paints or pieces of coloured paper to decorate the inside and outside of the card. Write your message on the back.

Secret Message

Cut a dog's body out of coloured paper, and glue it to the front of a folded piece of card. Draw and cut out the dog's head, and glue just the top part to the body.

Make a tiny envelope (pages 10–11), pop in a secret message, and tuck it under the dog's chin!

PUZZLE CARDS

The pictures on these cards are magically revealed when the pieces are put in the right order, or when the dots are joined together!

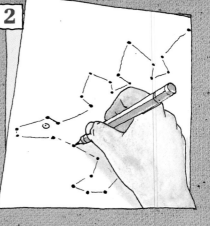

Dot-to-Dot

Lightly draw a simple design onto a piece of card, using a pencil.

Use a felt-tipped pen to mark clear dots along the pencil line.

Number the dots in the correct order. Rub out the pencil, and mount onto a piece of folded card.

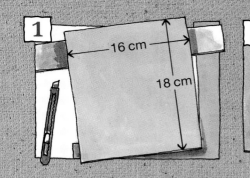

1 16 cm 18 cm

2 2 cm

Jigsaw card

Draw a rectangle measuring 18 x 16 cm onto a piece of thick card. Cut it out.

Draw a border 2 cm inside the edge of the card. Cut this border out, to make a frame.

3

4

Place the frame on another piece of card. Draw along the inside with a pencil, and cut this out.

Turn this piece of card into a picture, using paints or paper collage, then cut it into simple jigsaw pieces.

5

Fold a 32 x 18 cm piece of card in half, and glue the frame to the front. Send the card in an envelope, along with the jigsaw pieces.

18   •19
17   •20
21   •23   •24
22
26• •25
•28 29
27 •30 33 36
• • 38
37 •

POP-UP CARDS

These cards look terrific, and they're easy to make when you know how! You can change the picture to suit any kind of theme – just follow all the measurements given here.

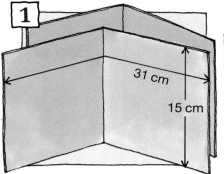

1

Take two pieces of thin card, each measuring 31 x 15 cm. Score and fold both pieces of card down the middle.

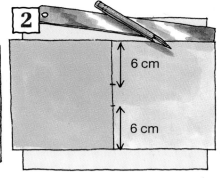

2

On one of the pieces, measure 6 cm along the fold from either edge, and mark the two points with a pencil.

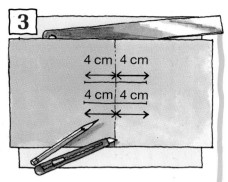

3

Draw an 8 cm line through each of these points (4 cm on either side of the fold line). Cut along both lines.

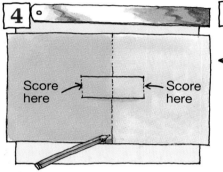

4

Now lightly score two lines between the cut lines, as shown.

5

Close and open the card, making the centre strip fold inwards.

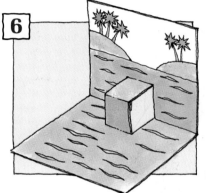

6

Decorate the background with paints or paper collage.

7

On a new piece of card, draw a pop-up shape – less than 11 cm high and 13 cm wide.

8

Cut out and decorate the pop-up shape. Glue it to the lower half of the centre strip, as shown.

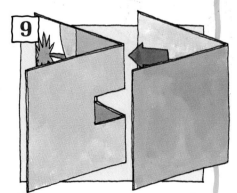

9

Glue the other piece of folded card to the back – but don't put any glue on the centre strip!

ZIG-ZAG CARDS

Fold, cut and unfold, and a whole herd of elephants appears! Try cutting out a different design, and you have a row of teddy bears, or a little train . . .

The tomato card has a special surprise tucked into its front pocket – a packet of seeds that grows into a beautiful plant!

1

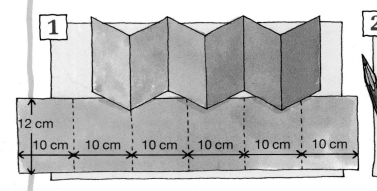

12 cm

10 cm | 10 cm | 10 cm | 10 cm | 10 cm | 10 cm

Take a strip of thin card, measuring 60 x 12 cm. Divide it into six 10 cm sections with a ruler and pencil. Score along the lines, then fold the card up into a zig-zag.

2

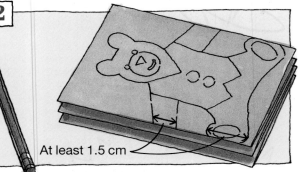

At least 1.5 cm

Draw your design onto the front of the folded strip. Make sure that the design touches both sides of the card for at least 1.5 cm, otherwise it will all fall to bits when you cut it out!

3

Cut out the design, then carefully unfold it again. Paint one side of the card, or glue down shapes cut from coloured paper. Write your message on the back of the card.

Say It With Seeds!

Buy a packet of seeds. Cut and fold a zig-zag (make it a bit bigger than the packet). Cut a pocket for the seeds from card, and glue it to the front.

On the inside, show what happens when you plant the seeds!

TOMATO

20

Pembroke Branch Tel. 6689575

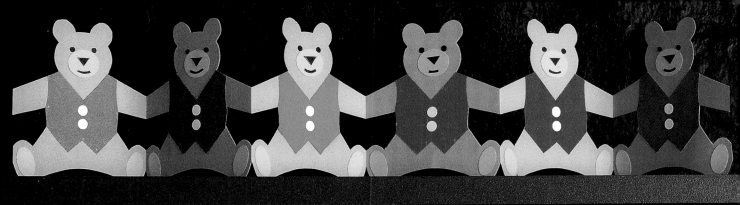

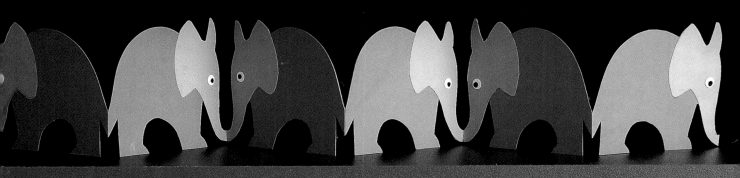

MOBILES

Yet another brilliant idea that's a lot simpler than it looks. This type of card is very eye-catching, since the mobile shape keeps swinging around in even the gentlest breeze.

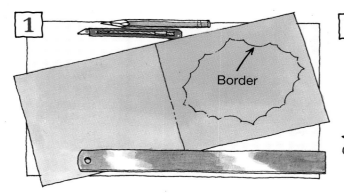

1

Cut out a rectangle of card, and score a line down the middle. Draw a border on the front – the cards in the photo should give you some ideas.

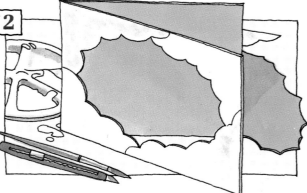

2

Cut out the part inside the border, and fold the card in half. Paint the front and insides of the card, or decorate them with paper shapes.

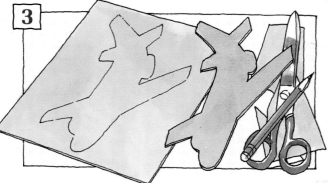

3

Cut out a shape from another piece of card. Make sure that it fits within the border. Draw around it to make a second shape, and cut this out, too.

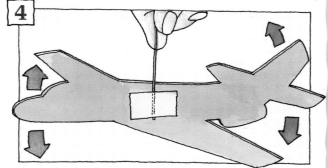

4

Cut a piece of thread, about 8 cm long. Tape it to one of the shapes – keep moving the position until the shape balances properly.

5

Glue the second shape over the first, so that the thread is trapped between them. Decorate both sides of the shape, with paints or paper collage.

6

Tape the top of the thread inside the front of the card. Check that the shape can swing around without touching the border.

MOVING PICTURES

Pull the tab, and watch the balloon glide across the sky!

For this design, you'll need one piece of card measuring 20 x 15 cm, and another measuring 42 x 16 cm. You'll also need to cut out a narrow strip, 26 cm long and 3 cm wide.

1

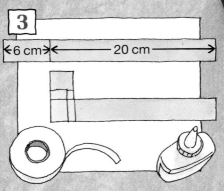

20 cm

3 cm

15 cm

Cut a curve across the smaller card, using a saucer as a guide. Leave 3 cm between the cut and the edges.

2

Decorate the card, avoiding the curve. Draw and decorate the balloon on spare card, and cut this out.

3

6 cm — 20 cm

Take the narrow strip, and cut it into two pieces. Glue the pieces into an 'L' shape, and tape over the join.

4

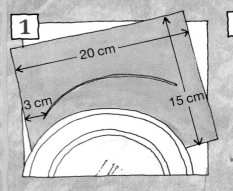

When the glue is dry, tuck the shorter length of the 'L' through the slot from behind, as shown in the picture.

5

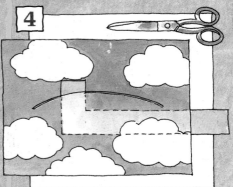

Glue the balloon to the top of the 'L' shape. Check that it moves freely when you pull the other end of the strip.

6

Fold the larger piece of card in half, and glue the decorated piece to the front. Don't put glue near the strip of card.

The winged horse flies across the sky in
the same way as the balloon.
You could also try drawing a
bird, a plane . . . or even
your favourite
superhero!

CARDS WITH FEET!

These cute 3-D cards can be folded flat for sending. The methods shown here can be adapted to make animals of all shapes and sizes – how about a tall giraffe, a plump hippo, or even a whole team of reindeer for Christmas?

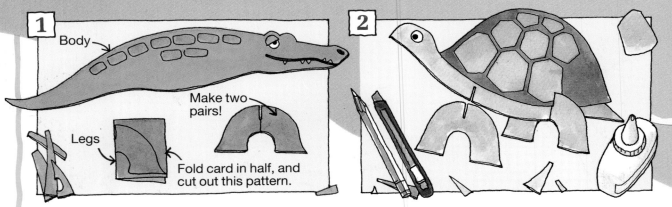

1 Body — Legs — Make two pairs! — Fold card in half, and cut out this pattern.

2

Crocodile and Turtle

Draw the turtle or crocodile's body onto stiff card, and cut it out. Make two pairs of legs as shown above.

Cut 1.5 cm slots along the bottom of the body, and into the tops of the legs. Decorate, and slot in the legs.

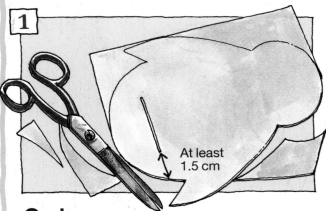

1 At least 1.5 cm

2 Fold over to make tail

Owl

Draw the body onto card, and cut it out. Cut a slot across the bottom half, leaving at least 1.5 cm between the slot and the edge of the card.

Cut out and fold a shape like the one above, for the feet and tail. Slot this through the body. Decorate the owl, using paints or paper collage.

Decorate one side of your animal
card, using paints or paper shapes.
Then write your message on the
other side – use a fountain pen, a
coloured felt-tip, or, best of all, a
gold or silver pen.

WINDOW CARDS

Stained-glass' cards look beautiful and mysterious – they're often made at Christmas time, but there's nothing to stop you sending them in spring, summer or autumn!

Cut out a 17 cm square of card. Draw a design onto the front, leaving at least 2 cm between it and the edge of the card. Leave 'bridges' of at least 1 cm between the holes.

Cut out the holes for the 'window-panes' with a craft knife. If you cut through a bridge by mistake, mend it with sticky tape.

Cut the windowpanes from pieces of coloured tissue or crêpe paper. Put glue on one side of the card, and stick down the pieces of tissue – trim them so that they don't overlap.

Fold a 39 x 19.5 cm piece of card in half. Draw a 2 cm border onto the front, and cut out the middle with a craft knife. Glue your stained-glass window to the back, as shown.

ZODIAC COLLAGE

Most of the cards in this book were decorated by gluing down pieces of coloured paper. However, you could also use old magazines, newspapers, tin foil, postcards, stamps, scraps of fabric and wallpaper, dried beans and pasta, flowers and grasses, shells, nuts and bolts . . . the possibilities are endless!

Here's how to make a zodiac card from collage. There are twelve designs to choose from – one for every star sign! Copy the shapes onto card, or ask an adult to enlarge them on a photocopier.

Cut and fold a piece of card – as big or as little as you like. Draw one of the zodiac signs onto the front. If you're using a photocopy, cut it out and glue it down.

Sort out the materials you're going to use. Put glue on the design, a little at a time, and gradually cover it with your materials. Leave it to dry before sending.

Capricorn

Aquarius

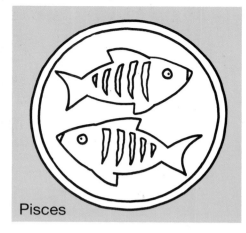
Pisces

Aries

Taurus

Gemini

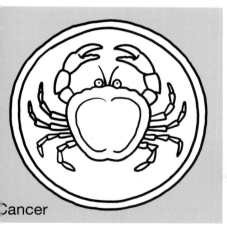
Cancer

Leo

Virgo

Libra

Scorpio

Sagittarius

CHRISTMAS CARDS

At Christmas time, when you need to make a big batch of cards, the best idea is to set up a printing press and go into mass-production!

For a few special people, try making the cat-in-a-stocking to hang on the tree – or turn the page to discover how to make a jolly Santa which jumps right out of the envelope!

Printed Cards

Follow the instructions for printing cards on pages 8–9. Print simple shapes, such as a tree, cracker, or a star.

While your printing kit is up and running, why not make your own wrapping paper – use wallpaper or brown parcel paper.

Print scraps of card to make gift tags. Make holes in the corners with a hole punch, and thread with ribbon.

Christmas Cat

Fold a piece of thin coloured card in half. Draw on the stocking shape, keeping the folded edge down one side. Cut it out.

Glue the edges of the stocking together, but leave the top open. Draw and cut out a cat from black card. Glue it into the stocking.

Decorate the card with bits of coloured paper. Tape a loop of ribbon to the back, and write your Christmas greeting underneath.

All kinds of simple Christmas shapes can be used for your prints and tree decorations. How about stars, snowmen, holly or angels?

Pop-up Santa

Copy the diagram (shown right) onto a piece of red card, using a pencil and ruler. Paint or decorate Santa's head, and the chimney section.

Score and fold the card inwards along the dotted lines, and tuck the Santa through the middle slit. The folded card should form a shape like the one shown in step 3.

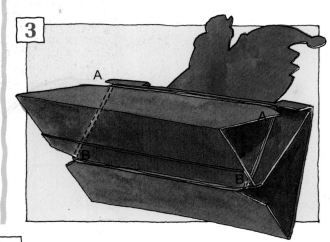

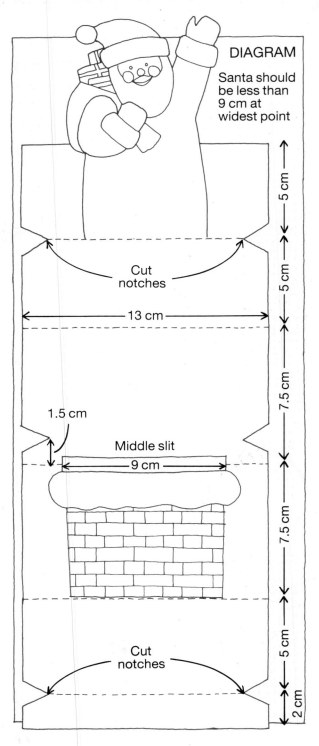

DIAGRAM

Santa should be less than 9 cm at widest point

Cut notches

13 cm

5 cm

5 cm

7.5 cm

1.5 cm

Middle slit
9 cm

7.5 cm

Cut notches

5 cm

2 cm

Loop one end of a rubber band over the notches at the back (A), and loop the opposite end over the notches at the bottom (B). This may look tricky, but it's very simple once you've got the hang of it!

4

To put the card into the envelope, gently squeeze the sides until it is flat.

When someone opens the envelope, the rubber band makes the Santa pop back up!

VALENTINE'S DAY

Here's a stylish Valentine's card to make for the one you love (don't forget to add a mysterious message on the back)!

Start by cutting out a rectangle of coloured card measuring 18 x 12 cm. Then take a piece of card in another colour, and cut out a square measuring 12 x 12 cm.

Try dangling a tiny heart on a piece of thread inside the main shape.

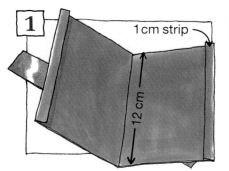

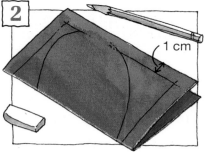

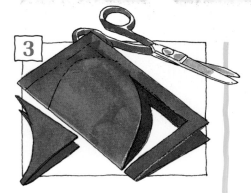

1 Score and fold the larger piece of card down the middle. Then score a 1 cm strip at each side, and fold the strips towards you.

2 Fold the smaller piece in half. Draw a border, 1 cm from the edges. Draw half of a heart shape, making the sides touch the border.

3 Cut out the area around the heart or, for a slightly different card, just cut out the heart. Both types are shown in the photo.

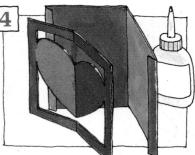

4 Glue the sides of the card to the folded strips on the larger card. Leave to dry before folding up again.

To make a pair of tiny hearts, just cut out a single heart from the middle of the folded smaller card.

EASTER CHICKS

When you open the top half of this Easter egg, a bright yellow chick hatches out!

You'll need a piece of card measuring 11 x 8 cm for each egg, and a 10 cm square of yellow card for the chick. You'll also need a paper-fastener to hold the egg together.

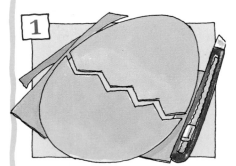

1 Draw an egg shape on coloured card, and cut it out. Cut a zig-zag across the middle.

If fluffy chicks don't appeal, how about a baby dinosaur?

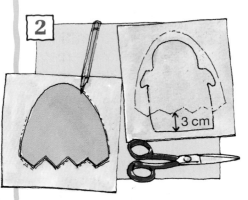

2 Place the top of the egg on the yellow card, and draw around it. Draw the chick inside the line, adding an extra 3 cm onto the bottom. Cut out the chick.

3 cm

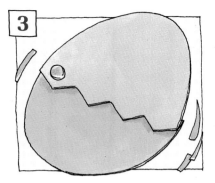

3

Overlap the two egg halves, and join them at one side with a paper-fastener. Close the egg, and trim the edges to make a neat shape.

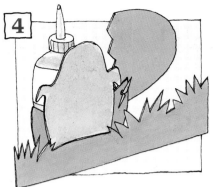

4

Glue the chick to the back of the bottom half of the egg. Cut out a strip of card 'grass', and glue this behind the bottom of the egg.

5

Cut and fold a piece of card, measuring 32 x 14 cm. Glue the grass strip and the bottom half of the egg to the front of the card.

Instead of step 5, you could make your egg stand up by itself – just glue a small piece of folded card to the back.

MORE IDEAS

You don't have to wait for a special occasion to send a card – it's a good way to keep in touch all year round!

Writing thank-you letters needn't be dull! Cut out a little card in the shape of the gift – all you need to do then is scribble your note of thanks on the back.

Moving house? Make some cards to let your friends know where your new home is!

Paper-fastener

Pack some plain postcards and your paints or felt-tips next time you go on holiday – home-made cards are a lot nicer than the ones you can buy from the tourist shops!

Pembroke Branch Tel. 6689575